RAISING THE BAR

Volume 5

Conversations with
Industry Leaders Who Go
ABOVE & BEYOND
For Their Customers

FEATURING:

Dr. Vidhya Kumaranayakam

Stefan Ciancio

Debbie Spector Weisman

Dan Hammick

Dmitry Badiarov

Jonny Cooper

Published by Authority Media Publishing Houston, TX

ISBN: 978-1-946694-49-2

Table of Contents

HIGH PERFORMANCE SUCCESS COACH

Dr Vidhya Kumaranayakam is a High Performance Success Coach and medical doctor, as well as a CEO, author, speaker, educator, wife, and mother to two young boys. Her incredible range of skills and knowledge help her to stand out in her field as a healer and coach – and rightly so. She has guided countless individuals, groups and companies to successes that they hadn't believed possible, helping them to reach their fullest potential and accomplish their goals, whether they be personal or professional.

She combines her experience as a leader and her healing abilities as a doctor with her skills as a coach and uses them to empower and awaken people. Following her guidance and with her support, Dr Vidhya's clients go on to transform their lives for the better. She helps them to see that their deepest desires and loftiest ambitions are achievable and works with them to set goals that will get them there. She knows from experience that hard work, self-discipline, and a commitment to good routines can get you where you want to go. In passing on this wisdom, she allows those she works with to understand what they really want out of life – and gives them the push they need to go out there and get it.

Conversation with Dr Vidhya Kumaranayakam

How did you find your purpose? What led you to this point?

Dr Vidhya: As with most spiritual awakenings, it happened when I felt like I had no choice but to really try to understand and listen to my intuition. Intuition is a beautiful mental faculty that human beings possess, and up until I sought to find my purpose, I had often unknowingly ignored it. But I have always been called upon to help people, and I am grateful to be a doctor and help people in that way. However, I am also a very spiritual person, and eventually I realised that I was being called on to focus more on being a Healer, which I thoroughly enjoy.

As for what led me to this point, I was involved in a car accident, which could have left me with some serious permanent injuries. Thankfully I was able to recover from my torn shoulder ligaments over the following six months. I was, however, taken aback by the emotional side of it, and in my determination not to develop PTSD I learned a lot about emotional intelligence and stability. This has become a huge passion of mine, and I do a lot of work on mind mastery these days as a result.

How did it feel when you became a mother?

Dr Vidhya: How I felt when I became a mother ties in to when I gained clarity over my soul mission. You see, I feel like I was born to be a mother and being one to my two young boys is an honour, a privilege, and the most important thing that I am doing and will ever do.

In response to my love of motherhood, I felt an impulse to learn about Mother Gaia and my connection to Mother Earth. This brought about a hugely powerful spiritual awakening and became a phenomenal part of what is now my H.E.A.R.T. system, which stands for Healing, Empowerment, Awakening, Rise and Thrive. I use this system to help people correct their course in life, rebuild after trauma, and manifest the life they want to live. I really feel as though this is a major part of my calling, and I have even changed the way I work in order to embrace the H.E.A.R.T. system more, so that my work is in alignment with my life purpose.

I saw online that you had helped pregnant entrepreneurs and those with toddlers to release themselves from toxic relationships and start their business. What was your process?

Dr Vidhya: I work with many mothers with young children and soon-to-be mothers who are interested in entrepreneurship, but who feel trapped by toxic relationships that are no longer serving them. Within just two weeks of starting group coaching with me, though, I helped a client to walk away from the relationships that were holding them back and start a business, and eventually to become a leader in their field.

To do this I follow my H.E.A.R.T. method and, in particular, guide my clients to focus on full moon rituals, gratitude journaling, and meditations that will help them release the toxicity from their soul missions. Interestingly enough, for one client I found that this toxicity seemed to stem back generations. It was evident she was carrying that negative energy with her, and that she needed to liberate herself in order to manifest the life she truly deserved.

I often find that entrepreneurs who have young children, babies, or are carers can find it particularly challenging to complete their profitable passion projects, but that they have no issue with commitment to their biggest goals. They often resonate with me as a mother with a baby and a toddler, because their bigger, holistic goals also tend to encompass the leadership role of parents, who want to consciously lead their children with emotional maturity. Using the universal laws, they want to help their children thrive in any environment, manifest the life they want, and take inspired action. As parents, that is the greatest gift we can give.

How can the readers get a similar result? What would be the steps they need to take?

Dr Vidhya: In order to manifest the life you want for yourself and your children, and to thrive in your business, too, you need to focus on the life you want in detail. Visualise your ideal life to epic instrumental movie music and write out your life movie with you as the star in as much detail as possible, using all of your senses.

When you are visualising, it's important not to focus on the past, because it is done. However, if there are negative belief patterns, stories or toxic people that keep coming up and recurring, then clearly, they need to be addressed. Remember that what you resist persists. We need to work to understand the karmic lessons that the universal law of cause and effect is teaching us and seek to understand them within this lifetime. Once you have learned them, you can begin to move forwards.

Journaling can help with this, by helping you to get out onto paper the low vibrational emotions that no longer serve you. You can also do rituals to cleanse these emotions using the powerful energy of the full moon. By having self-awareness and understanding all of the ways you can balance your emotions, you can learn to view your life from an outside perspective and come to understand that you do not need to have fear. You should focus on faith, rather than fear. Fear just means lack of knowledge – so gain knowledge and know. Remember, though, that often this knowledge is spiritual, as opposed to random news or trivia.

Other things you can do to help you manifest your ideal life include stopping watching the news altogether. All it does is feed your fears, and it is not reflective of all the good things happening in the world. You should also make an effort to review the company you keep, cut any ties that no longer serve you, and replace them with things that do. Ultimately, this will require you to focus on your relationship with yourself, and to grow through your comfort zone and into the seemingly "unknown". That is where the life you want lies!

Setting aside time every day to meditate, visualise your life movie and practise gratitude is extremely important, too. So, ensure you set up a daily appointment with yourself to work on all of this and study your mindset. It doesn't matter whether it's early morning, midday or bedtime, although early morning rituals and meditations can be particularly powerful. Recognise that this will be the most important appointment you will have in your day, because it has the power to help you correct the course of your whole life. Just ensure you give it the time, energy and respect it deserves. Setting aside that time is not a luxury, but a necessary part of self-care, self-trust, and self-love, and it will help you to heal, balance and restore the foundation of the self that is known as the root chakra.

It's also important to focus on balance, especially of the masculine and feminine energies which we all have, regardless of the gender we identify with. These energies are spiritual, not physical, but this is very often mistaken by most people – including by me in the past!

Clearly, these steps are a lot to think about. So, if you want to make the best of them, then find a mentor or coach to really go deep on this with you. It is important for all the pillars of your life (health, wealth, relationships, spirituality, etc.) that you do.

What has most surprised you about your journey so far?

Dr Vidhya: That I am being loved for being my authentic self, most of all by myself! I don't know why I waited so long to listen to my intuition.

I've also been surprised by how the universe will just pull the rug from under your feet the longer you ignore your purpose. But so often there are so many signs and messages along the way, and that final pull of the rug is a beautiful thing that is done to protect you and ensure you get to where you need to go. You might not have moved if the universe hadn't lit the fire under you to get you moving.

What mistakes did you make and how could you have avoided them?

Dr Vidhya: There are few mistakes in life, except when you don't follow the light that shows itself to you, and you continue on without it. Having a scarcity mindset about money, relationships, self, and other things can hold you back in a similar way. However, you can avoid this by listening to your intuition rather than others' opinions of you, ensuring you have healthy boundaries, and not being a people pleaser. Focus instead on self-mastery, and this will be reflected in all aspects of your life.

It's also important that you communicate what you need to make you happy and healthy with yourself and your loved ones. This will help you to heal the past and move forwards and stop you from muting your light. You are being called on to use your individuality and powers of creativity to be a beacon of hope. Take the risk, because people are waiting for your service.

Shine your light bright and go for it. Take that leap of faith, and you will build a plane on the way down that will sky-rocket you back up! This is something I often remind myself and my inner child of, and in the past, I have also written it in letters to myself as part of a healing ritual. I suggest you try it, too.

What have people's reactions been like towards you? What are the highlights and how did you deal with any negative reactions?

Dr Vidhya: Peoples' reactions have been very positive and encouraging, and many have told me they wish they had done the same as me. At one point, I even got a message from some old friends who were struggling in the dark after they saw one of my Facebook lives, to tell me that my work was helping them. I hadn't spoken to them in almost 10 years! And that is the law of attraction in practise.

I see any negative comments I get as good things, which act as little tests to check that I still follow my intuitions and am able to release the toxicity which no longer serves me.

What challenges have you faced and how did you overcome them?

Dr Vidhya: The car accident I was in and the emotional impact of it were a huge hurdle for me to try to jump over. I have also dealt with toxic relationships in the past, which didn't help with me being a people pleaser. However, now that I have balanced my masculine and feminine energies and done so much work on self-mastery, this is no longer a problem.

More recently, I had to contend with going through pregnancy and labour through a postnatal period with my own "lockdown" when my first born and I had to isolate to protect him from getting any infections after some birth complications resulting in sepsis and a stay in ITU. Thankfully we thrived through this thanks to all I researched and learned about emotional health, mind-body connection and mindset which I now teach in my coaching, courses and consultations. I had to isolate for four months in total and I was determined to not get postnatal depression during this difficult period – so instead I started my business and published a book!

How do you plan on further growing your business?

Dr Vidhya: I will be throwing myself into everything from courses to masterminds, retreats, seminars, new books and speaking engagements, to help me get my message and teachings of self-healing, self-empowerment and self-leadership out there, as well as continuing my private clinic in Healing. It's a pleasure to serve.

Where can the readers find you?

Dr Vidhya: Readers can find out more about me and my work by getting in touch via email at diamondsuccessmindset@gmail.com. They can also join the FREE Diamond Success Mindset Facebook group, where they can access free books and journals to help them navigate their hero(ine) journey in this school of life. Join at:

www.Facebook.com/groups/576794759672148

About Dr Vidhya Kumaranayakam

Upon graduating from St Bartholomew's Hospital and The Royal London Medical School, Dr Vidhya Kumaranayakam went on to train in a number of specialised areas, including Psychiatry, Emergency Medicine and Rehabilitation. Thanks to the breadth of her knowledge and her innate determination, she consistently climbed the ladder, and she was at one time an NHS Mental Health Clinical Director and a Partner in a successful NHS GP practice.

However, while struggling with both the physical and mental impact of a car accident, Dr Vidhya came to learn a lot about emotional intelligence. She realised during this time that her true calling lay beyond just the medical side of healing. Now, as a High Performance Success Coach, she draws upon her wide-ranging professional background to help high achievers come into their full potential, teaching them how to manifest the life they truly want to live.

And her work doesn't stop there. Over the years her incredible work ethic and drive have seen her become a global leader in Human Potential and Holistic Health, a consultant with the Proctor Gallagher Institute, the founder and CEO of a media company, and a published author.

WEBSITE
www.DrVidhya.com

FACEBOOK
https://bit.ly/DrVFacebook

TWITTER
Twitter.com/DrVidhyak

INSTAGRAM
https://bit.ly/DrVidhyaInsta

LINKEDIN
LinkedIn.com/in/DrVidhya

YOUTUBE
https://bit.ly/DrVidhyaYoutube

PINTEREST MARKETING COACH

Online marketer and coach Stefan Ciancio has made a big name for himself within his niche, focusing as he does on Pinterest marketing strategies. He knows from experience that, when leveraged correctly, this free platform can help entrepreneurs to up their organic traffic by the millions, generate leads and sales, and help them to establish their brand and audience, all without breaking the bank. In fact, since starting his business from nothing back in 2015, he has helped countless clients do just that!

As a coach, he is knowledgeable and motivational, believing that if he is able to help people get even one percent further in their business, then he has an obligation to do so. As well as advising clients on how to market effectively using Pinterest, he also offers product launching and affiliate marketing services. Through his determination to succeed, he has found exactly what works for him and his business.

As a result, he has generated seven figures in sales, regularly makes upwards of five figures a month, and lives and works wherever he wants. His goal is to help as many other people as possible find the freedom and fulfilment that he has as an entrepreneur.

Conversation with Stefan Ciancio

How did you find your purpose? What led you to this point?

Stefan Ciancio: I thought that, surely, I had to have a higher purpose than sitting in a cubicle from nine to five, five days a week. In fact, I even wrote a blog post about it back in 2013, in which I asked myself and my readers "could this really be it?" Little did I know, though, was that what I was doing then was *not* all there was, and that just five years later, I would be an accomplished online business owner with a whole plethora of high-income skills. Little did I know that I would eventually be my own boss, have generated seven figures in sales, connected with like-minded online entrepreneurs from all over the world, spoken at marketing events in multiple countries, and much more...

Little did I know that I would end up building a business and lifestyle I would love, and finally be living up to my true potential. I found that my purpose was to build an online business while traveling the world, and empowering others by helping them understand *all* of their options away from formal education, including the beauty of self-education, and starting and growing various full time online businesses and side hustles.

I was led to this point from what I mentioned above: sitting in a cubicle from nine-to-five with everyone around me constantly miserable, mumbling things like "the weekend was too short" or counting down the days to retirement. What a horrible way to live. I knew I was not going to be doomed to that same fate. My desire to succeed – which was fuelled by seeing others online already successful and through finding comfort in online communities of aspiring entrepreneurs – really helped me to find the path I wanted to go down.

How did your biggest achievements make you feel?

Stefan Ciancio: There are so many achievements I'm proud of! One of the biggest was the day that I quit my job, and only my roommate/co-worker knew what I was about to do. I remember waiting for my boss to come in that day, and I was both nervous and excited. My boss was busy that morning; his office door was closed until at least 10:30AM. Eventually, though, I went in, and while my boss seemed a little shocked, he also seemed pretty excited for me. He did ask me to stay on for a few extra weeks, though, as they were short staffed.

A co-worker came into my cubicle later in the day, surprised at my decision. I guess word had spread. It was one of the happiest and most liberating moments in my life. I felt like I was about to embark on a new adventure, and I did. It felt like I was taking a bet on myself and thinking about the endless possibilities was amazing.

Then, about three to four months after I quit, I hit my first five figure profit month. It was an incredible feeling of accomplishment, and validation that I had made the right decision. In the first few weeks after I left my job, my initial feelings had been a combination of excitement and fear. I had almost no money saved. But the fact of the matter is that this made me tough. It forced me to sink or swim, and to develop the skills I needed to never have to go back to a day job. Some people think they would be helpless if they left their nine-to-five, but with the right knowledge and mindset, you could actually end up in the opposite position. By this point in my career, I have developed countless skills and gained a ton of knowledge that will allow me to keep earning money through my business, and not have to rely on a nine-to-five job. So that fear made me resilient. It made me confident that I could do it.

Another achievement I'm proud of is the day that I moved to New York City to be an entrepreneur full time. Part of the reason I had wanted to become my own boss was so I would have the freedom to choose where I wanted to live and work from. Moving to NYC in 2016 as a full-time online entrepreneur gave me a huge feeling of accomplishment, as well as excitement for things to come. It symbolized taking back control of my life and being in the driver's seat, by saying "I am going to go and work from here", and actually being able to do it on a whim.

Then, eventually, I crossed seven figures in sales. Now, revenue is not profit, but there really is something magical about hitting that seven-figure benchmark.

Off the back of all of these other achievements, I was asked to speak at an online marketing event in 2017 for the first time. It was just in front of a small group of around 50 people, but it felt great. It made me take stock of the fact that, just two years prior, I had been working a nine-to-five job and feeling miserable. Now I was in Portugal among amazing, like-minded individuals, speaking to them about my knowledge and my journey. It was such a humbling experience.

I saw online that you had helped a friend get to five figures a month and work with one of the biggest names in internet marketing. What was your process?

Stefan Ciancio: Well, what I told him to do was develop a high-income skill – copywriting – and then focus entirely on getting good at that skill and finding people you can help. He would go on Upwork and try to get clients, and it was slow for the first month or so. He was discouraged and wanted to give up, but I told him to keep going, and make sure he was reaching out to at least five people per day.

Soon enough, he had landed steady work with a few clients… and now he has a full time, five-figure-per-month, location independent position with a prominent online agency owner, and he continues to go onward and upward.

He did what you are supposed to do: find the thing that works and then grow it. Do not deviate and try to do 40,000 things. This is something that I personally still struggle with as an entrepreneur – the shiny object syndrome or FOMO. I want to have my hand in a ton of different things. Unfortunately, though, this approach just spreads you so thin that you can't really focus on the one or two (or in some cases three) things that, if you actually spend all your time growing them, will get you better results and genuine success.

Another client whose success I helped cultivate was a woman called Tatiana, who had been on my email list for quite some time. We got around to talking on Facebook one day, and she was telling me about a skill she had developed, using Facebook groups to get easy leads. I knew that this skill was something people would pay money to learn, because it could help people grow their own businesses by getting leads in the same way.

So, we did a product launch of a video course which presented a case study of her results and the exact instructions of her method. The launch did 1,000+ sales, and so even though we only sold it for around $10, she now had a business. I told her to focus on keeping up to date on that method, and then helping others succeed with it.

How can the readers get a similar result? What would be the steps they need to take?

Stefan Ciancio: One of the easiest ways to grow an online business is to sell your expertise or knowledge. If you can get someone just one percent further along than they were, you can help them greatly, and I believe you have an obligation to do that. You can also use webinars to get people warmed up and ready to work with you. In fact, they are a huge part of what allows me to deliver my services.

All you really need to get started online is to learn a high-income skill, and either teach it or sell your services. For example, copywriting may be one of the highest income skills of all time, and learning Facebook ads is another. If you become proficient in these skills, you can do extremely well.

Take that friend I mentioned before, who learned copywriting using entirely free resources and a couple of books. He had been down on his luck, but by skilling up and putting himself out there, he managed to land himself a five figure-a-month gig as a copywriter for a prominent agency – a job he can do on his computer from anywhere in the world.

So, the lesson is to learn a high income skill, and either sell the knowledge or offer the services. A big part of my business is selling my knowledge, and another is making entrepreneurs' lives easier, through software products that help business owners scale, save time, and perform tasks more easily, among other things.

What has most surprised you about your journey so far?

Stefan Ciancio: I am surprised by how fast things have changed (and continue to change) in the digital world. The skillsets evolve fast and keeping up is a very important part of the game. There are a few fundamentals that don't change, but the mediums do. For example, email marketing is not nearly as prominent as it once was, and it's more about social media and SMS now. That may change again soon – it's always changing. So, you need to learn to adapt or you *will* fall behind.

What mistakes did you make and how could you have avoided them?

Stefan Ciancio: One of the biggest mistakes that I still make to this day is spreading myself too thin, although overall I have gotten better. Sometimes I think that, by spreading myself over five to ten different projects at once, one or two of them will be bound to work. However, when you do this you end up dividing your time, which stops you from giving each project the nurturing it needs to actually grow.

A good analogy for this is to think of each project as a seed that you plant in a pot, and your time as the water needed for the seed to grow. Your time (water) is limited. If you divide the water across ten plants equally, they only get a little bit each, and this won't be enough for them to grow into their full potential. But, if you spread all that water (time) across just one, two, or maybe three plants (projects), you will have a small handful of big successful plants (projects), as opposed to ten failures.

Another mistake that I made in the beginning was not understanding the insane cost of trying to do everything myself. Outsourcing is now a very important part of my business, and I recommend that others try and outsource as much as possible as well. A small team goes a long way.

What have people's reactions been like towards you? What are the highlights and how did you deal with any negative reactions?

Stefan Ciancio: It's always interesting when you tell people you're an entrepreneur. The two most common responses are usually either excitement and respect, or something along the lines of "oh..." With the latter, you can tell they are thinking that "entrepreneur" is just a codeword for jobless bum.

But I don't care what people think anymore because I know I've made it, and I don't have anything to prove. However, I do still remember that, when I quit my job, I was a little shocked at the scepticism and disbelief I got from my old engineer co-workers when I told them I was starting an online business. I wish people were a little bit more open-minded.

What challenges have you faced and how did you overcome them?

Stefan Ciancio: When I quit my job, I had thousands of dollars in the bank – and owed tens of thousands of dollars in debt. But I overcame that by focusing on what worked. Within four months of quitting my day job, I had upped my income to over five figures per month, and I kept it there for a while. I had only quit my job because I had found one income stream that had proven itself, and I knew that with an extra 45 hours in my week, I could focus entirely on that and get it to the point of replacing my job income (and then some). So, focusing on the thing that is proven to work is my advice here.

Other challenges I faced – that I suspect many other entrepreneurs face – is ridicule and doubt from friends and family. I remember a quote from a short video for entrepreneurs that I saw on Facebook, which said: "in the end, your success will speak for itself". So, I stopped caring about the naysayers and focused entirely on building my own success. I was also able to join many online communities of like-minded people from all around the world who were encouraging, empowering and on the same path as me. The joy of this, coupled with the excitement of being on a path with people from all over, really kept me going. So, this is definitely a great piece of advice: try to find people who fit your narrative. Find people who are encouraging and empowering, and when you do you will find that your journey becomes easier. When we confine ourselves to our existing, disempowering echo chambers, we limit our growth and lose sight of what we really want.

Ironically enough, two of my friends were so inspired in the end by what I had done, that they both ended up quitting their day jobs as well to become full time entrepreneurs.

How do you plan on further growing your business?

Stefan Ciancio: I will continue to focus on what's working. For example, I run a few core courses that help others learn proven methods for growing their own businesses and overall making their lives easier. I will also keep going with my work on Webinarkit and Growth Commander, which are software programmes that make peoples' businesses more automated, easier to run, and increase their leads and sales.

Where can the readers find you?

Stefan Ciancio: Readers can find out more about me at StefanCiancio.com, and about my business at ActionTakingBlogger.com. Those interested in my work on Webinarkit and Growth Commander can also check out GetWebinarKit.com/live and GrowthCommander.com.

About Stefan Ciancio

After studying Mechanical Engineering at the University of Connecticut, Pinterest Marketing Coach and Online Marketer Stefan Ciancio spent three years working in a nine-to-five job as an engineer. However, he soon realised that this career path was not his calling.

When money worries encouraged him to pick up a side-hustle, Stefan realised that he had a talent for online marketing. All he was doing was up-selling items on eBay that he had purchased at a bargain price, but he found he was making a lot of money doing it. It was his successes here that led him to his lightbulb moment: that the one thing everyone needs to succeed online is traffic.

In 2015 he finally left his job to become an online entrepreneur full-time, helping people to up their traffic by the millions. His specialty is Pinterest marketing strategies, because of the ease with which this free platform allows users to grow their organic traffic, leads, sales, brands and audience.

Stefan is currently the co-founder and co-owner of several businesses, as well as the President and CEO of the Master Growth Marketing Agency. His day-to-day revolves around supercharging the traffic of all types of businesses, as well as product launching, affiliate marketing, and coaching others to be experts in these fields, too. While it may sound as though he has a lot on his plate, his life is freer and more fulfilled now than it has ever been. He has definitely found his calling.

WEBSITE
ActionTakingBlogger.com

PINTEREST
Pinterest.com/ActionTakingBlogger

YOUTUBE
YouTube.com/c/ActionTakingBloggerStefanCiancio
/featured

DISCOVERING THE POWER OF YOUR DREAMS

On the surface, Debbie Spector Weisman's life checked all the boxes: happily married, two children, co-owner of a successful business, money in the bank. But inside she was prone to the nagging thought that something was missing, a feeling that sometimes spiraled into depression. She took things personally, whether it was personal or not. She became more sensitive and beat herself up over more and more things. She could have continued living this way until she had a dream that dramatically shifted her life.

Debbie's dream was her deep inner voice talking to her. It told her that she had been living her life in fear, too timid to speak her mind, afraid to explore her feelings. With this insight, she took steps to break out of the shell she had created, which resulted in improved communication and relationships with those around her. She also realized that while her job gave her income, it wasn't her true passion. The more she studied dreams, the more she became convinced that her new mission was to help others transform their circumstances by understanding and working with their dreams. This became her new passion, as she came to learn from her own experience that we hold the answers to most of our problems in our subconscious and that dreams are the gateway to that knowledge.

For the past eight years, Debbie has provided one-on-one coaching to dreamers internationally as a Certified Dream-Life Coach. Debbie's ideal client is someone who feels stuck and needs help figuring out where they go next. Often these are people experiencing life changes—divorce, retirement, empty nest, loss of job—and their uncertainty is reflected in their dreams. By showing them how to understand the hidden messages in their dreams, Debbie's coaching helps them rediscover their purpose and passion, shows them how to process anger, worry and fear, lose the feeling of victimhood and learn to love themselves unconditionally.

Debbie believes that everyone should pay attention to their dreams and she is helping spread their importance through her weekly podcast Dream Power Radio and TV show The Dream Power Show.

Conversation with Debbie Spector Weisman

Why should I remember my dreams?

Debbie Spector Weisman: We spend about a third of our lives sleeping. Wouldn't you want to know what's going on in that part of your life?

This may sound a little wonky but bear with me. Dreams originate in our subconscious, the part of the brain that is active while we're sleeping. Unlike our prefrontal cortex, the part of our brain that controls our waking thoughts, the subconscious is not filled with the thousands of random negative thoughts that flood us all day long. The messages we get at night are unfiltered. Some are trivial; some are profound. They can be simple recaps of our day, fanciful flights to magical lands, strange stories that leave us bewildered, or incidents and images that can give us insights into how to solve problems and offer solutions on how to better live our daytime lives. When we become expert at remembering our dreams, we can program ourselves to have them answer specific questions we ask right before bedtime.

We humans have been paying attention to our dreams for as long as we've walked on Earth. Evidence of dreams have been found in 7,000-year-old relics found in China and India. The Greeks used dreams for healing and built temples specifically made for this purpose. The Iroquois Nation was a dreaming society, meeting in circles to discuss their dreams and using them to plan their lives. Even in the early years of the United States it was common for families to discuss their dreams at their breakfast tables.

Then there are the examples of dreams that have had direct impact on our lives. Elias Howe perfected his invention of the sewing machine because of a dream. Albert Einstein got the idea for the Theory of Relativity from a dream. Dmitri Mendeleev created the Periodic Table of the Elements as a result of his dream. Countless books, movies and songs got their starts from the dreams of their creators. The list goes on and on.

Dreams can also be fun. One of the most common dreams is the flying dream where the dreamer soars through the sky to destinations real or fanciful. Often people dream of feeling satisfied after eating magnificent feasts or giant bowls of ice cream and not gain a single ounce. If you realized that you could access your dreams, wouldn't you want to know how to do that?

I don't dream, so I have no dreams to remember.

Debbie Spector Weisman: If you don't believe dreams are important, you're not likely to remember them and that's why it may appear that you don't dream. However, sleep researchers have confirmed that we all dream, anywhere from four to nine dreams a night, depending on our sleep cycles. The only exceptions may be people taking opiates or other types of prescription drugs that interfere with the REM cycle, the time when most dreaming occurs.

How can I remember my dreams?

Debbie Spector Weisman: Here's my 7-step method for remembering dreams.

BEFORE YOU GO TO BED

1. Create a serene environment: It's hard to sort out your dreams when your bedroom is a mess. Declutter your sleeping space. Make sure your room is neat and clean and you don't have piles of stuff stacked up on your night table. Close your closet doors. Cover your mirrors or make sure they're far away from your bed. Turn off–or better yet–unplug all electrical devices. Heighten your senses by sleeping on soft, comfortable sheets and

spraying a welcoming scent like lavender on your pillow. The idea is to consider your place of slumber a sacred spot of honor.

2. Cut out the alcohol: Don't put your brain at a disadvantage. A sober brain is more likely to remember dreams.

3. Prepare to remember: Keep a journal and pen or pencil nearby so you can write down your dream when you wake up. If you're technologically friendly, there are also several handy dream apps available for recording your dreams.

4. Make a dream declaration: Right before you drift off to sleep, literally say to yourself, "Tonight, I am going to remember my dreams." Putting that intention out there is a reminder to your brain to pay attention.

BEFORE YOU WAKE UP

5. Don't move a muscle: This one may be hard to remember, but it's a key factor in dream remembrance. Dreams live in our subconscious and short-term memory, which is why we often forget we ever had them. But there's a golden moment to capture them, and that's in

that fuzzy time between sleep and that full awake feeling. When you start to feel as if you're rising out of your sleep, stay exactly where you are and focus on what you remember about your dream. Repeat this to yourself several times as you stay in the same position. It's important at this point not to move, as any physical gestures can jolt you into full consciousness and make that memory fade away completely.

AFTER YOU WAKE UP

6. Write it down: As soon as you're sure you've got the dream in your head, grab that journal or recording device and record it. This is important for two reasons. If you don't get it down, you're likely to forget it by the time you're up and about. Also, the act of writing or speaking about the dream helps you to remember other details that might have slipped your mind when you first woke up. Writing it down also gives you the space to remember how you feel about the dream - a very important component in understanding what your dream means.

7. Tell a friend: Retelling the dream to another person really cements the dream in your mind. Talking about it may also spark thoughts as to its meaning.

If after all this, you still find it hard to remember your dreams, take a big deep breath and relax. Chances are all this is a new process for you and changing a long-held habit takes time and patience. Give yourself permission to be forgetful. In time, if you're committed to remembering your dreams, there will be a morning when you wake up with a delightful surprise–a remembered dream!

What do I do with the dreams after I write them down?

Debbie Spector Weisman: Unfortunately, dreams don't come to us in easy-to-understand stories. They're filled with symbols and the key to decoding the dream is to figure out what those symbols represent. When you're awake, re-read the dream aloud several times until you have a clear understanding of it. Take note of the symbols. Use a dream dictionary to look up the standard meaning of symbols and see if the answers resonate with you. Ask yourself how these symbols relate to what's going on in your life.

See if you can weave all this information together to create an interpretation that makes sense to you.

I have crazy images in my dreams. What do they mean?

Debbie Spector Weisman: One of the reasons people don't pay attention to their dreams is their weirdness. In fact, the word weird comes from the Old English word wyrd, which means fate, fortune, and destiny—another sign pointing to the importance of dreams. So, it pays to take the time to work on understanding them. One tip that helps is to look at each symbol one at a time and ask yourself: What does this mean to me? You might be surprised at the answers.

The dream I credit with changing my life consisted of one word: codpiece. How weird is that? A codpiece is a medieval garment used by men to cover their genital area. It took me a while to figure out how it related to me, but I'm glad I took the time to do it. I wrote a detailed explanation of how I decoded this dream in the book *Chicken Soup for the Soul: Dreams and Premonitions*.

If you're really stuck on the meaning of a symbol, don't despair. You can contact me for a full analysis of its meaning and how the dream relates to you and your life.

What about nightmares? Why should I remember them?

Debbie Spector Weisman: I like to quote the late dream master Jeremy Taylor who said, "All dreams reflect inborn creativity and the ability to face and solve life's problems." Nightmares are no exception. In fact, I believe nightmares are your subconscious' way of telling you that the message in this dream is so important it's scaring you, so you'll remember and pay attention to it. Often, a nightmare will give you clues to a problem you're facing in your daytime life.

Because they contain scary images and frightful incidents, it's natural to want to forget a nightmare. But I believe that a nightmare could actually be the best thing that can happen to you. If you take the time to decode the dream and figure out the message that's being sent, you can learn things about yourself you might not know otherwise. You can get answers to issues that are bothering you and resolving them could give you peace of mind.

I had a client who called me in a panic because she had a dream in which her baby died. At the time she was pregnant and had a small child and she was scared this was a prediction that something terrible was about to happen. Since dreams are symbolic, I had a strong feeling the dream wasn't about the impending demise of her real child. Babies in dreams usually symbolize innocence or new beginnings and death could symbolize the end of a phase or situation. When I asked her how the dream related to her life, she revealed that she was starting a new business with a new partner, about whom she had doubts. The dream confirmed her thoughts that the partnership was ultimately doomed and that it was better to "let this new baby die" and focus on other, better, business opportunities in front of her.

The outbreak of Covid-19 across the world resulted in an increase in people remembering their dreams. Most of them were nightmares, with frightening images of virus balls, bugs, masks, flying insects, being stuck in crowds and the like. While most of these nightmares reflected anxiety and fears about the disease, some also reflected other concerns of the dreamer. For example, dreams of bugs could mean that something "is bugging you" and figuring out what that is might resolve an issue in your life. A mask might represent a "false face" you or someone you know is presenting. But like all nightmares, once you dig down to its meaning, the alarming aspects of the dream go away.

I have the same dream over and over. What does that mean?

Debbie Spector Weisman: Recurring dreams are very common. In short, they represent a persistent problem or situation in your life. If you can figure out how to resolve that problem or situation, you will stop having those dreams.

What do I do if don't know how to take action on a dream?

Debbie Spector Weisman: That's where the services of a Dream-Life Coach like me comes in. Often a dream will reveal a self-limiting belief like fear, lack of self-confidence or unrsesolved anger, and is related to situations that may leave you feeling stuck and unable to make or carry out important life issues.

My work with dreamers is twofold. First, I help the person understand their dream. I have the dreamer recite the dream in detail. Then I ask questions about the dream. We go over each symbol and incident in the dream, getting a sense of what those items mean to the dreamer. I don't tell her what they mean, as the dream has more meaning when the dreamer reaches her own conclusions. I use my experience and expertise to lead her to that understanding.

The next stage is getting a clear idea of how the dream relates to the dreamer's life. Most people who seek my services come to me with disturbing or confusing dreams that correlate to an incident or a feeling that's affecting them at that time. They look to the dream to give them guidance or insight on how to handle that.

Having that knowledge leads to the next step, taking action on the dream. Usually this means making a decision or doing something that often is easier said than done. For example, someone who has a dream that reveals they're better off leaving their job may be reluctant to make a move if they're not sure what they want to do next. Or someone whose dream shows them they have to stand up for themselves may be afraid to make their feelings known.

Through various techniques, I help the dreamer break through what's holding her back, enabling her to carry out the action hinted at in the dream. The results are often life-changing and can include an increase in self-confidence, self-assurance, clarity of purpose and an increased passion for life.

One note of caution: These results are not automatic. The process takes commitment, perseverance, and work. But for those willing to put in the effort, the results can be transformational.

How can readers find out more about Debbie Spector Weisman and what she does?

Debbie Spector Weisman: If you want to learn more, go to my website: TheDreamCoach.net. You'll find information about dreams, my blogs, my story, my eBook, and a quiz to determine if you could benefit from a Dream-Life Coach. I also offer a complementary Dream Discovery Session available through the website.

I also host a weekly podcast, *Dream Power Radio* apple.co.\3519yAu, and monthly TV show *The Dream Power Show*, available on Roku and Amazon Fire, that features expert interviews with dream workers and those dedicated to empowering peoples' lives.

About Debbie Spector Weisman

Debbie Spector Weisman, The Dream Coach, is the host of the podcast *Dream Power Radio* and *The Dream Power Show* on Roku and Amazon Fire. She has incorporated the knowledge gleaned from her professional work and as a wife and mother into her Dream-Life Coaching practice. In addition to her private coaching work, Debbie has been the co-owner of a film and video production company which was instrumental in the production of dozens of films including the groundbreaking film *What the Bleep Do We Know!?*, and the spiritual documentary *Dreaming*

Heaven. Debbie is also the best-selling author of over 20 young adult novels, including five of the original books in the popular *Sweet Valley High* series.

She credits her dream work with inspiring her to return to writing after a twenty-year hiatus. Her most recent books include *101 Dream Dates: How to Say I Love You to the Most Important Person in Your Life --You!* and the best-seller *It Came Out of My Vagina, Now What?!*, co-written with Betsy Chasse. She is also featured in the books *Chicken Soup for The Soul: Dreams and Premonitions, My Creative Thoughts, Recipes for Living, Careers from the Kitchen Table, Dancing in the Unknown,* and *Dreams That Change Our Lives*. Debbie is a member of the International Association for the Advancement of Dreams and The Holistic Chamber of Commerce.

WEBSITE
TheDreamCoach.net

EMAIL
debbie@thedreamcoach.net

LOCATION
New York

FACEBOOK
Facebook.com/DreamWithDebbie

TWITTER

Twitter.com/DreamWithDebbie

OTHER

LinkedIn.com/in/TheDreamCoach

Using SMS for Business

In today's ever-changing technology-driven society, the average local business owner might feel like they are running on a treadmill, going hard but going nowhere fast. When I was a kid, there were no personal computers, no internet, and no mobile devices except on television shows like *Star Trek*, which were based centuries into the future. Now all those things are a reality and have changed the way business works and thrives. Our world is linked up and connected with access to it all thanks to the mobile revolution walking around in the palm of our hands.

This revolution continues, but simple, long-lasting principles of business and marketing continue. In current times, a business must be able to communicate with its customers quickly and efficiently and stand out from the clutter and overwhelm of pop-ups on websites, click-to-actions all over the web, and ads in traditional media like the TV, radio, and local newspapers, which are going digital or by the wayside. One thing for certain is that almost everyone has a mobile device that they are glued to and carry with them everywhere they go. My business helps businesses and organizations build Mobile Databases through different promotions to communicate with their clients or groups quickly and easily using mobile multimedia SMS texting services. The clients we service range from restaurants to realtors and developers, retail stores to property managers, churches and schools to sports teams, all to communicate directly to the mobile device that everyone has with them all the time.

Conversation with Dan Hammick

What types of businesses do you help, and how do you help them?

Dan Hammick: I would say small to midsized businesses that operate on a local level are best suited to using SMS services inside their organizations. We like to find out what problems the business is trying to resolve, and if there are solutions that SMS services can provide. So, we don't just say, "This is the greatest thing since sliced bread, and you need this, and it doesn't cost that much, and you will love it and thank me later."

I think that businesses are tired of all that. With this current pandemic situation and shutdowns, many businesses are shell shocked or on the borderline of never recovering because they never expected something like this. So, with that in mind, simple examples of a problem for a sector of the economy are restaurants with large dining spaces that are forced to close. So, they need to pivot, have a customer database that they can use to easily communicate with customers, and an online ordering system (not Uber Eats or Skip the Dishes or other online ordering and delivery app).

The platform we provide allows us to build a local restaurant's customer base using simple marketing materials placed on tables, menus, host entrance, and online on their website and social media. They offer an incentive for opting into a database and receive rewards and special offers available only for those who sign up. All this info is then tracked and can be segmented into different lists.

We help our clients send their marketing messages with trackable offers or communicate notices or updates, or whatever they want to communicate. So, when COVID hit, a business like a restaurant could have informed their customers that they were closed, when they planned to reopen, takeout or curbside pickup is available, the precautions they were taking, and a myriad of other pieces of information they needed to share. Sadly, many businesses did not have a way to communicate directly to their customers and will suffer because of it.

Another problem is driving more customers through on slower nights, since this causes food waste and the losses incurred from that. Having a database and the ability to send out an SMS blast with some incentives can fill some seats or generate online orders, bringing more customers and more cash flow.

One more problem is getting more repeat business from their customers. Statistics say it costs 5x more to obtain a new customer than to keep an existing one, and an existing customer is 20-to 65% more likely to buy again from a business. So, it is much more profitable to keep customers, and you can only do this with effective follow-up and regular communications.

We help solve this by using a system of incentives for being a special VIC/VIP member. We can then create contests, polls, special offers, and other promotion strategies to drive more engagement and bring people in more often. A great benefit of this system is that people actually respond to their marketing messages because they have joined the club and they have the offers right in hand on their mobile devices, as opposed to some messaging in a newspaper that they forgot to clip, or a radio spot that they heard but didn't make a note of and away it went from their minds.

An SMS message directly to their mobile devices is with them almost all the time. Just as a side note SMS messages are checked by 98% of people within a minute or two. Think that can be beaten by any other medium? Nothing that I know of comes close.

Another industry I help is a service business like golf courses. The biggest problem they have is they are selling time spots and the clock is always ticking. So, after they have done their marketing and booked a tee time, they need to make sure the golfers show up on time so they can keep the course full and not waste or lose spots. They also need to have a backup list to quickly fill any last-minute cancelations. Every time they miss a slot, they lose revenue that can never be regained.

One of our SMS systems gives the course an automated way of setting up Tee Time reminders, so the players can confirm their slots. This frees up time for staff to book more players or deal with other things in the pro shop. I find it very annoying when I'm inside a business and get interrupted by a phone call and the store staff take the call and make you wait, don't you?

This same service works for any business that has defined appointment times, like a doctor, dentist, spa, or hair salon. The principal solution is hands-free appointment reminders to ensure your seats are full, revenue keeps coming in, and has appointment reminders automated.

Another industry we service is the real estate industry from a sales side, marketing and building a list of contacts, and the property management side of the business. We have a system for using SMS to show a home virtually with people being able to receive information via a SMS message with link to a video tour, photos, and details about the listing or project without having to actually talk to anyone yet. Many people want to check something before contacting the agent first and waiting for a call back. This eliminates the need to print flyers and hope they don't get wet, blow away, or run out of them.

The benefit for the agent is capturing the contact data in a noninvasive manner and being able to communicate via 2-way SMS chat built into our system and give out information and filter out hot leads from lookey lue's and ask questions to better help clients find what they are looking for. The agent can then follow up on auto pilot with leads in the system.

On the other end of the real estate industry are property management services. This could be a shopping mall where they need to communicate with the tenants, staff, or staff of tenants. Many do use SMS already, but I have found they are doing this with their own personal cell phones, which is not really something they should be doing for personal and privacy issues.

Another way SMS could be used is for an apartment block manager who can use the system for rent reminders, happenings in the building from maintenance issues, fire, or emergencies, package deliveries or other things to communicate to tenants. Most operate with terrible communications as they may post a notice on the front door or elevator or even on the tenants' door, taking time, paper, ink and the strong possibility that not everyone will see it. Who wants to be having a shower and the water gets cut off and you missed the memo? Or the window washers showed up and you're caught streaking through your own space because you missed the memo. Having our system will eliminate the communications problems and keep happier tenants which keep the place full and rents coming in.

The same system can help rent out units faster by letting tenants know units are available and getting in-house referrals and giving virtual tours for prospective tenants. This can save advertising costs and time as many tenants may know others who may want to live in the building.

Several other types of organizations that can benefit from SMS services not from a marketing perspective, but just pure communications are groups, such as sports teams and clubs, churches, and schools, who all need a way to en masse deliver messages to the group, or even on an individual basis. SMS is the most used method of communication with some 12 billion sent a day around the globe. It is here to stay, and we help our clients set up systems to meet their needs.

What's one of the biggest mistakes you see local businesses making when marketing online?

Dan Hammick: By far the biggest mistake I see is businesses not building a database of customers and marketing and communicating to them consistently. Now this could be an email list which for a long time has been the typical way in the web revolution of collecting that database, but the consistency of sending out messaging on a regular basis is lacking for the most part. Also, just to note on average, email open rates are around 22%.

A lot of businesses have this mastered, and as the online marketers always say, the money is in the list, and it is if you do it right. Our platform utilizes the SMS system and can add email capture and messaging combined for double the effectiveness. We can send out both email and SMS messaging and monitor, track, and evaluate to refine the messaging to help grow our client's business have a super valuable asset, a customer list for easy and consistent communication.

What's one strategy a local business should include in their online marketing that their competition probably isn't doing?

Dan Hammick: There are many strategies a business should be doing in their online marketing, but the one that seems to me to be lacking is building a database of customers and then communicating with them regularly. This does not mean just blasting them with offers but provide information about things like updates on new staff, new ways to use the products or services, changes to hours of operation, updates to policies like in the current COVID situation for rules and standards that the business has implemented.

In my experience, many businesses ignore building a database, because they believe since they have a physical location, customers already know where it is, when it is open, and will always come back. The lockdown situation is devastating for those businesses because they don't have a system in place to communicate quickly and easily, and customers have not been able to come by the business as usual.

One of the hardest hit industries is restaurants that had to close and then could reopen only for takeout, delivery, or curbside pickup. Many had no way to broadcast this directly, so business dropped off dramatically or worse, the business has now closed permanently. This could have been avoided if they had a system and a customer database in place to update their customers. Now I am a little biased because this is a service my business provides to businesses, but the strategy is sound whether they use our service or another company's service.

What led you to help local businesses with their marketing?

Dan Hammick: Well, it started when I was in my late teens and had my first business, which was a cleanup service for new construction. Most of my friends from school were from families that owned a business or were real estate developers. I was, and still am, very inquisitive about business and how businesses work since most of my family had regular jobs and made a living by trading hours for dollars. I was taking classes in college for a business degree, and we had a Q&A day in one of our classes. Everyone in the class asked questions about micro vs. macroeconomics, accounting questions, just textbook type questions.

I asked the professor if he owned or had ever owned a business, and he said, "No." I asked if he was rich or financially independent and was a teacher for the pure enjoyment of helping others get into business and thrive. He answered, "No" again. The others in the class wondered why I asked such pointed questions, and didn't get what I was after, which was to learn from someone who has or is doing it in the real world of business as an entrepreneur.

I thanked him for being honest in his answers, closed up my book, packed up and left. I knew he and school were great in theory, but how was I going to learn something from someone who had never done it, who just had studied business and had a job trading hour for dollars? I kept working in and on my business from that point and sought out my friends' parents who were business owners on how they did things and how business actually worked. Since then, I have studied, learned, and asked a lot of questions of business owners while growing, building, succeeding, and failing in the University of Hard Knocks.

I have also taken courses in school and now online to further grow and learn and help others to grow their business. When the digital age came along in the early 2000s, I was starting to use a computer and getting a new business going. I had to learn how to get the business setup in local listings and didn't have the funds to pay someone, so I went about another learning curve. I eventually figured it out, but it took a lot of time and frustration. Once I got things set up, others were asking me to do it for them, and that started my journey to helping businesses with their online marketing.

In retrospect, it was a blessing, but I wouldn't advise anyone to go down that rabbit hole themselves. I have learned now that as a businessperson, to grow your business faster, get the help so you don't waste time. You will never recoup time, but you can recoup the money to pay other experts.

How can business owners find out more about you and how you can help?

Dan Hammick: There are quite a few channels to get in touch with me and the business. We are a virtual business and work with clients almost anywhere mobile SMS texting services are available, which pretty much covers the globe.

I also have written a Book on SMS Marketing that people can request a Free Digital version or buy a Physical copy on the website. The book goes into more detail about using SMS technology, things to note and avoid, and some of the basics of using SMS campaigns and communications to a group.

About Dan Hammick

Dan is an entrepreneur at heart, starting since a teenager. As an avid reader of over 500 business books and student of what makes a successful business tick, an athlete for life, and freedom lover, Dan has studied business and technology trends both in the classroom and in the trenches that affect the marketplace.

Having spent most of the last decade living abroad, consulting businesses on trends and establishing tech into businesses, learning Spanish, and Founding a Charity to establish a Disc Golf League for schools in Mexico, he delved into SMS technology and started a service for businesses to utilize its benefits for communication to its customers.

Today Dan is studying for an MBA with Heriot Watt for more knowledge running his charity and consulting businesses, as well as constantly learning as much as possible about the online world, business automation using technology, and real world business integration.

WEBSITE
www.UseSMSMedia.com

EMAIL
info@usesmsmedia.com

LOCATION
Puerto Vallarta, Mexico

Tel: 250-999-7010 can/usa
52-322-171-3687 mexico

VIOLIN DESIGNER AND MENTOR

Dmitry Badiarov is world-renowned as a designer of beautiful, concert grade violins, the person behind the revival on the Violoncello da spalla, and because of his past career as a classical musician. Though sadly he is now unable to play the violin, his life still very much revolves around music. These days, his focus is on creating instruments that incorporate the ancient secrets of acoustics, and helping other aspiring designers do the same. However, he knows that design is only one part of the story, and that when it comes to making instruments, it is important to leave a legacy. In order to do so, you have to learn how to market yourself effectively.

Having learned everything he could about digital marketing from countless masterclasses and courses, he now passes on his wisdom to those hoping to offer something original and innovative to the world of classical music. He has helped countless dreamers to make a name for themselves in the world of instrument design and has kept ancient the tradition of fine violin making alive in the modern age.

Conversation with Dmitry Badiarov

How did you find your purpose? What led you to this point?

Dmitry Badiarov: Before I became a mentor, I was a concert violinist and a designer of original violins made using the ancient secrets of acoustics. I got to travel to some amazing places doing what I did, from my native Russia to Merida in Spain and many other beautiful locations, on trips specifically dedicated to my research and as a member of the baroque music ensemble Le Petite Bande.

I spent many years building up my design career, too. It wasn't easy to decipher the secrets of the ancient musical masters, but I knew that I wanted the violins I made to tell a story and pay homage to the deep roots of classical music. It took a lot of time, effort and money, and I struggled with debt on a number of occasions, but thankfully my efforts eventually paid off.

Unfortunately, between 2010 and 2013 my career went into a nosedive, and in 2013, I suffered a massive, near-lethal stroke that left me paralysed down my left side. I was told by doctors that I would be lucky if I could still walk, before they broke the heart-breaking news that I was unlikely to ever play the violin again. I was devastated and wanted nothing more than to die.

My wife, also a professional musician, was thankfully there by my side to support me through those dark days. She said: "What if you share your knowledge? Imagine how many people you could help!"

So, from June 2016 I started attending countless masterminds and courses on online marketing and education, learning how to market my skills and use them to teach other aspiring instrument makers how to make something of themselves. We live in a world where factory-made instruments flood the markets, and I want to uplift those offering something original and creative.

I still design handmade, one-of-a-kind violins for world famous, international musicians, but I am unable to play myself anymore, and so I have had to adapt. These days, my life still revolves around music, but more as an ambassador to the ancient traditions, helping other instrument makers to create their legacy at bench and keep these cultural traditions alive.

How did it feel when you took your instrument making business to six figures?

Dmitry Badiarov: It felt surreal! I have been designing violins since the 1990s from my workshop in Brussels, Belgium. But it was only after I began educating myself on the power of online marketing in 2013 that my business really got off the ground. Then, in 2018, I finally did it – within the first two months of the new year, my business passed that six figure milestone. After spending so many years in debt at the start of my career, I couldn't believe that I'd managed to make such a success of myself, and all from doing what I loved.

Off the back of this financial success, I was invited to speak at a digital marketing conference in London. It was a fantastic experience. I was proud and happy and excited to share my knowledge with a new crowd of people. But beyond that I was also inspired, knowing that I and other classical music lovers would not have to watch a 500-year-old tradition of fine violin making die a slow death.

I saw online that you had helped a client launch an internationally renowned workshop in just 12 months. What was your process?

Dmitry Badiarov: Yes, his name was Oleg Ivanyschuk, a Ukrainian violin maker based in Spain, and not only was he able to launch an internationally renowned workshop, but he also got featured in the national news three times and was attracting customers from all around the world, all in his first year of business.

When he started working with me, I first went through the ancient acoustic design system with him, to help ensure that the sound he wanted to achieve would be obtained with 100 percent clarity. Then, we worked on getting great visual appeal, and after that we looked at the all-important pricing strategy and completely changed that.

These are three crucial components of a successful instrument making business. Once we had those fixed, we could start to market him and his business in a way that generated a stream of customers and made it easier for musicians to buy from him.

How can the readers get a similar result? What would be the steps they need to take?

Dmitry Badiarov: While it is important to take a good look at your marketing, pricing, and the quality of your products or services, it is also extremely important that you do not let external limitations decide your life.

At the start of my career, I was faced with people telling me that I would never make something of myself, and I also struggled with lack of money and time. But these things are surmountable – you just have to be willing to give it your all and make sacrifices if you really have to.

So, use your internal powers to decide that you want to succeed, say "*yes*" to the things you want to achieve, and then go on to figure out how you can do it.

What has most surprised you about your journey so far?

Dmitry Badiarov: The fact that the tools and systems that successful people use are relatively simple to use yourself. I've come to realise that we all have access to similar information and plenty of opportunities to put ourselves out into the world using the same sorts of methods. But then, why is it that not everybody is successful? How come some people can make a name for themselves and some people can't?

I think it has to do with the fact that, surprisingly, many people have little or no faith in themselves and their abilities. Really, it's a mindset thing. Because if two people have the same skills and experience but only one has the money and fame to show for it, then there really can be only one explanation.

You won't put yourself out there and keep working towards your goals if you don't believe in yourself. You have to be determined and tenacious, and that's just not possible if you don't think you can get very far.

What mistakes did you make and how could you have avoided them?

Dmitry Badiarov: I have made some choices throughout my career that I think some would call mistakes, but I do not think of them as such. For example, back in 1990, I borrowed $1,000 from relatives and friends – which was the equivalent of a one bedroom flat in St. Petersburg at the time – in order to buy a set of chisels and planes to start my violin making shop. I was told I would be unable to repay my debt, that I was a fool, but I absolutely believed this was the right thing to do.

So, a lot of my riskier decisions are ones that I have never doubted or regretted – I would not call them mistakes. There is, however, just one exception.

The biggest mistake I have made in my time was telling a mentor "I want to do this my way." Mentors see what we don't see and that is why we go to them, to learn and grow from their wisdom. By not listening to my mentor, I lost my business a lot of money.

What have people's reactions been like towards you? What are the highlights and how did you deal with any negative reactions?

Dmitry Badiarov: People's reactions are often either very kind or very harsh, and these two extremes are usually particularly pronounced online. People have a strange way online of assuming things about what I do or who I am, without really knowing or caring about the truth. I have even been told that I am a leach who is "taking advantage of poor people," and I do not really understand why. But I know that we do not know what's going on in other people's lives, and that many people act like that because they perhaps do not have an amazing life. So, I try to share love, even when it's not easy.

Thankfully, though, my clients are always good to me and I know that I have helped to change people's lives. "Thanks to you," one client told me, "I am now living my dream."

What challenges have you faced and how did you overcome them?

Dmitry Badiarov: Back when I bought those instrument making tools for a $1,000, I had to deal with friends and family telling me that I had lost my mind, that I would never be able to repay my debt. I wasn't sure yet whether they were wrong or right. But there was this tiny voice in my mind, telling me: "Come on! This is your dream!"

There was also a time more recently when people took my new interest in online marketing and education almost as a betrayal, and they could not accept the new me. I think this has to do with the fact that, in music, people are not easily forgiven for changing directions or adapting to new realities. Take the musicians on the sinking Titanic as a case in point. They chose to make music until the very last moment, without even attempting to save their own lives. This is a trait the director captured perfectly, because music becomes an identity for so many people. And so people expected me to stay stagnant, even in spite of my stroke. It was painful, but I chose to be faithful to my purpose.

In both cases, I just had to go with my gut and trust my instincts. I understand what I am meant to do and will continue doing what it takes to achieve my goals, no matter what anyone else says or thinks.

How do you plan on further growing your business?

Dmitry Badiarov: One positive thing that 2020 has done for us is teach us a lot about what can be done online, particularly in the field of marketing.

So, I want to take what I have learned during this time and use it to help more and more aspiring instrument makers create successful businesses that they love.

Where can the readers find you?

Dmitry Badiarov: To find out more, readers can view my website at BadiarovViolins.com, and I am also on LinkedIn, Facebook and YouTube.

About Dmitry Badiarov

Known to clients and customers alike as the Ambassador to Ancient Traditions, Dmitry Badiarov is all about keeping the cultural tradition of violin making alive and well in the twenty-first century. He himself has been making beautiful, original violins for world famous musicians for decades, after working tirelessly at finding a way to incorporate the ancient secrets of acoustics into his designs. However, in order to prevent the designs from fading into obscurity, he realised that entrepreneurial skills would be required.

He threw himself into learning all about online marketing in the wake of this revelation, and as a result he has been able to spread his wisdom further afield. He currently sells his violins to renowned musicians and teaches some of the most promising aspiring instrument makers the tricks of the trade.

He first generated six figures in sales back in 2018 and has continued to thrive ever since, thanks to his approach to marketing and his original outlook on classical music. In September 2019 he also went on to become an Academy Award-winning speaker and has been featured in The Strad magazine and on the Dutch television programme *How It's Done*.

WEBSITE
BadiarovViolins.com

EMAIL
dmitry@badiarovviolins.com

FACEBOOK
Facebook.com/DmitryBadiarov

YOUTUBE
YouTube.com/c/Badiarovviolins-Custom-Made-Fine-Instruments-Sale

LINKEDIN
LinkedIn.com/in/Dmitry-Badiarov-Mentor-Violin-Maker-Award-Winning-Speaker/

JONNY HATES MARKETING

For someone who really, really hates marketing, Jonny Cooper has managed to build himself an impressive reputation for helping coaches, trainers and therapists attract more of their ideal clients more quickly. He's been in the game for a long time and, while he has experienced some pretty crushing blows and life-altering failures, he has always persevered and come back fighting. Using non-traditional marketing strategies that are tried, tested and just a little bit ingenious, Jonny shows his clients how to get their businesses out in front of the right people and draw them in.

The spark that ignited Jonny's latest business endeavour, Jonny Hates Marketing, was the realisation that many coaches and trainers struggle to make ends meet. So, he wanted to help the people trying to make a difference in the lives of others by teaching them the tips and tricks of the marketing trade and has taken many entrepreneurs from small-time to stand-outs in their field.

Conversation with Jonny Cooper

How did you find your purpose? What led you to this point?

Jonny Cooper: I remember exactly when I believed I'd never have to work another day in my life - after a multimillion-pound business sale. It was a consultancy I'd built up over nearly a decade that was making eight figures, and when I sold it to a public company I thought my days of hard work were over. I couldn't have been more wrong! The deal had set out that I would get paid in stages, but after just 18 months the buyer went bust, meaning I only got a small fraction of the money.

Unfortunately, I had already moved into a £1.2 million house and was driving flashy cars. But I was living this lavish lifestyle on yet-to-be-earned money, and just four years after the sale I was in £500,000 of debt. I ended up having to declare myself bankrupt and spent the next several years flailing around with a lack of focus. But I knew how to build a good business – I just had to recover from my "vagueness virus" and figure out how to put my skills back into action.

Ultimately, I realised that if I was struggling with a lack of purpose and direction, then other coaches must be, too. I had started to notice that a lot of online experts were suffering from a lack of business know-how and struggling to make ends meet, so I decided that this was the group that I wanted to help.

How did it feel when you grew your business to eight figures and sold it?

Jonny Cooper: It felt fantastic – like I'd conquered the world! I had started that business from scratch myself and managed to take it to these amazing heights. At the time of the sale, it had 200 staff across eight offices and a turnover of £10 million. It gave me an unbelievable sense of achievement, let me tell you.

And then, when the opportunity came for me to sell it, I was thrilled. Not only had I built this incredible enterprise, but it actually looked as though it had set me up for life. When the purchaser company collapsed owing me millions, that was pretty hard to take. Especially as, tasting the promise of eight figures written into the contract, I really believed I had achieved a dream that only a few can reach.

I saw online that you now help coaches and therapists create more impact in the world. What was your process?

Jonny Cooper: It started with the realization that the really big, expensive problem a lot of coaches and therapists have is that they have no clear vision of what they actually do for their clients, or even who their ideal clients should be. These are people who have skills and experience in their field, and who have the potential to do big things. But it's no good them offering life-changing services if the right people don't know they exist.

I know from experience what it's like to not have a clear direction, and I went through a phase of saying yes to any old client because I didn't know how to attract the right ones. It doesn't lead to success or an impressive client list. It just leads to you being overworked, underpaid and unfulfilled.

So, I offer my clients the tips, tricks and strategies for pulling in the right people that I know work. And I don't just help to get them off the ground. In fact, plenty of my clients are now fully-fledged success stories, with a laser-like focus and wealthy clients. I give them the opportunity to make the impact they deserve to make, and all it really takes is guidance and some business acumen.

How can the readers get a similar result? What would be the steps they need to take?

Jonny Cooper: Any successful business has to start with a deep understanding of who you serve, and what they're suffering from that you can help then with. It sounds simple enough, but there are plenty of business owners out there who don't have these basics down.

If you're just launching your great idea, start by first identifying *what* is the big, expensive problem your products and services can solve in people's lives. Then, work out *who* are the wealthiest kind of people who would benefit from that. And finally, decide *how* you're going to deliver your product or services as the valuable, reassuringly expensive solution your ideal clients need.

What has most surprised you about your journey so far?

Jonny Cooper: I'm constantly surprised that I'm still alive, happy and thriving! I've had a lot of ups and downs in my professional life and helluva lot of crazy adventures outside of business. I never really thought I'd get to the point where I'd be settled in what I'm doing and feeling completely fulfilled doing it.

As a child, I wanted to be an airline pilot, but fell down at the first hurdle thanks to my poor eyesight. Later, I started my professional life as a musician, and while it made for a fun few years in my early twenties, it didn't make me a whole lot of money. As well as playing piano, I am also an international racing driver, and have driven some amazing cars in some amazing places.

With all that under my belt and behind me, I have to say I am happy to be at a point in my life where I'm making seven figures doing work I find freeing and enjoyable, and giving my family the comfortable life they deserve.

What mistakes did you make and how could you have avoided them?

Jonny Cooper: I spent far too much time focusing on lazy pleasures, chasing them when I should have been concentrating on the more important things like financial stability and a fulfilling work-life balance. But you know, avoiding those blunders would have required me to be someone else, and not me. I only have the perspective I do now because I have learned, grown, and been forced to pick myself back up after some painful knock-backs.

Spending so much money after my business deal led me to reckon with some particularly difficult consequences. I had been promised the money but that wasn't the same as having it in my bank account. Living the life of a millionaire before I had actually become one was a massive mistake, but one that I just wasn't sensible enough to avoid. I wanted to drive a Ferrari and live in luxury after my biggest business success to date, and back then, I'm not sure anything could have stopped me.

What have people's reactions been like towards you? What are the highlights and how did you deal with any negative reactions?

Jonny Cooper: Most people have been entirely indifferent to me throughout my life, and the only thing that really changed as I gathered some modest success was that more people probably decided they didn't like me. And that's fine. I have no strong feelings about how anyone reacts to me, positive or negative, and the thought of trying to control that never crosses my mind.

What challenges have you faced and how did you overcome them?

Jonny Cooper: Having no money was definitely the biggest challenge I have ever faced and filing for bankruptcy was an incredibly difficult thing to have to do. I'd already lived a life on little money when I was a professional pianist, but after going into business I never thought I would have to go through that again. It was particularly crushing after such immense successes. My business had been making millions, and I had felt as though I was made for life when I sold it.

I overcame that, though, by knuckling down and figuring out how to put my skills and experience to good use again. I realised that I could solve more problems for more people using everything I know about business and marketing, and have people pay me to do that.

How do you plan on further growing your business?

Jonny Cooper: I'm going to keep on doing the things that I do best, which are solving problems and growing businesses using innovative and elegant approaches to marketing. I am always working to discover the simplest ways to succeed in our industry, without having to spend crazy amounts of money or run myself into the ground. I've gotten results using straightforward, streamlined processes, and I am continually looking to improve for both myself and my clients.

At the moment, I'm just venturing into a ground-breaking attack on expanding my reach through Facebook advertising, to create global impact and transformation.

Where can the readers find you?

Jonny Cooper: Readers can find out more about my story and what I do by visiting

JonnyHatesMarketing.com/.

They can also join the legendary Jonny Hates Marketing Facebook group

at Facebook.com/groups/JonnyHatesMarketing.

About Jonny Cooper

Having worked for several years as a professional musician and an international racing driver, Jonny Cooper went into the world of business in order to make a better life for himself. He grew his first enterprise into an incredible eight figure business, then exited and founded his latest endeavor, Jonny Hates Marketing.

He had realised that so many skillful, experienced entrepreneurs were not making the impact they were capable of due entirely to a lack of marketing knowledge. The business coaching services that he offers now are there to help trainers, therapists and coaches build up their client base and turn their skills into marketable assets.

After many years of building up his own businesses from scratch and turning them into success stories, he is well placed to offer guidance and advice to those struggling. He has already managed to turn around the lives of so many entrepreneurs, and his goal is to keep on going. In fact, he is well on his way to hitting his target of impacting the lives of 1,000,000 professionals by 2025, both through his services as a coach and his book, *Jonny Hates Marketing: 99 Ways To Get Your Ideal Clients Chasing You Without Spending A Penny On Advertising, Working Like A Dog Or Losing Your Mind.*

WEBSITE
JonnyHatesMarketing.com

EMAIL
jonny@jonnyhates.marketing

BUSINESS FACEBOOK
Facebook.com/JonnyCooperGlobal

FACEBOOK GROUP
Facebook.com/groups/JonnyHatesMarketing

LINKEDIN
LinkedIn.com/in/JonnyCooper

www.ingramcontent.com/pod-product-compliance
Lightning Source LLC
LaVergne TN
LVHW010107110826
845155LV00028B/518

* 9 7 8 1 9 4 6 6 9 4 4 9 2 *